AF334709

LAKE SYSTEMS

LAKE SYSTEMS

Tougher Disguises Press

Oakland, 2004

Cynthia Sailers

LAKE SYSTEMS

Grateful acknowledgement is given to the editors of the journals in which some of these poems first appeared: *Barn(v.), pompom, Secret Swan, Litvert.com, Stolen Island Review, A Very Small Tiger,* and especially Duration Press for publishing part of *Lake Systems* as an e-book, *A New Season.* Special gratitude goes to Tanya Brolaski, Brydie McPherson, Stephanie Young, Barbara Joan Tiger Bass, and Julia Bloch for their careful reading, encouragement and support.

Design & Layout: James Meetze

Distributed by: Small Press Distribution
                  www.spdbooks.org
                  email: orders@spdbooks.org

9 8 7 6 5 4 3 2 1

Tougher Disguises Press
P.O. Box 9033
Oakland, CA 94613
www.tougherdisguises.com

ISBN 0-9740167-3-X

Table of Contents

10 AMERICANS

9

LAKE SYSTEMS

17

INHUMANE

61

For James Harris
1927–1987

AMERICANS^{10}

We are all Greeks who might have called ourselves
a wooden panel, who might have been a painted bronze.
But we must have found our identities were hidden
in schools and colleges, and we must have found
that our genealogies were rhetorical. If not, what
am I now if in the clearing? Today we saw the seagulls
extend the outer limits, to secrete their own pattern.
Held in the atmosphere of a winter. Like when I was
a boy yearning for verticality, an echo lost to all
echoes. En route to those weak spots or to those
masked as men. Who came between a thin line and
falling ice. Who vocalized a paradise in bald summary
and were failed, in the formations of remembering,
in front of a loaded wall of paintings. Who belong
to a country of flags waving. For when someone turns
the faucet on. When I decided to love. When someone
is lying awake, I can not help the maternal other.
I can not help dwelling between the clock and the bed.
To rest in our pipe dream. The materials are in my fingertips.
In a one room apartment. We can lock ourselves up in violence.

If it wasn't for the civic solidarity that brings us back
together again it was a force of habit. We were always
arguing and breaking apart. We were always making
the dogs fight. And often, we were on the pier,
hollering about the exact color of the dog. "He is white.
He is highly educated." But here we were, without a reason.
Where we imagine ourselves posed. Where we are
revisionary. Can we not try to change but measure
the effects of change? Too often we were Western
intellectuals who speak of the city as we know it.
And often we were voting for impersonality, devouring
what made it into the picture. Of another season,
conjuring up the Island fog that becomes our moral
understanding. Then we were often writing to the cows
on the interstate, spelling out a question. When we couldn't
help them from nearing their end, and when we lost
the thought of being heralded. We spoke out against those
Western intellectuals and then we were speaking out
against ourselves, and the discomforts of our island, and
individualist waterways. As something very quiet interrupts
the dream. A train has come. This might be my insomnia.
To be thrown out with the dirty bathwater. So that we
are not an ocean, holding up our hands in the streets.

We imagine ourselves outsiders, in a continuous strain
of going public. We remember ourselves in American
society, in the context of our houses. We were
impressionists when we understood impressions better.
Who we are when we walk down the strip. The more
numerous we are, we imagine ourselves surrounded by
blue sky, and that we will find ourselves more than we did
yesterday. Walking across the park, across a courtyard
looking back on past events, loving animals, with human
discourses that seem certain to be there, in nameless things,
in ethics, in conversations. I was born to a man and a machine.
This is certainly not what we had imagined in coming out of
our houses and believing in the ethics of lakes.
We feed its condition and when we are there with them
we have the feeling that we do not relate to one another,
repeating our condition that "this is the misfortune of living
with yourself." When I imagine myself endlessly emptying
into us, I believe in the differences in our ways.
In an obituary about who we are and who we should be.
We are their contemporaries, we are not classical figures
named for our common sense. We are not named for our good
behavior, in a hemisphere we found to be a blank screen
onto which we project all our American fantasies.

Elsewhere we misrepresented the architecture, not
so much the corners but the soft shapes. It has become
easier to imitate now that our elsewhere has a great
food system for inhabitants, and an elsewhere has
a town. Here we were surrounded by beauty. It gives
us security, it is giving us a code word for serious
capitalism. It is not easy to resist, this standard of all
places, where we ate some chickens. And where
we felt this new area had brought us to the irreducible,
that the land makes up its mind and wins. With no warning
we came to call ourselves derogatory. This was
the elsewhere we came to when we ate chickens.
And where the ethics were a gentle melancholy across the lake.
The social and biographical characteristics of our friends
who remained eating the chickens, and who were wondering
why all the contemptuous indifference. We would have
liked nothing better than to see why we had become
acquainted with ethical systems and why we saw visitors
come to the land to see gray birds banked in a sea
of ratios. How they just sit there, giving us an odd sense
of continuing as we were looking out at them.
And just as they are not individuals they roamed the
Island. And then the people would see why they were
the humanities and why everything around them is helpless.

And yet we were the individuals who do not relate
to one another. When we find there's a desire
to be crowded, to be all the numbers, or the observers
who would see in the faces that those faces were not
the answer. That those faces only pointed to
the amphitheatre of the mind in an hour of romantic
enthusiasm. If only we were immigrated, if only
we were knowledge, not like gardens, but underneath
it all, a shape of equal vividness, constrained by the one
thought we thought we wanted. A tracing of ourselves
against the beauty of lakes and grasses and colonial houses.
To be brushed along and kept close to the skin.
We were prepared to admit a solution for the lower forms
of life, for the seductive centuries and a break with
the past. And yet we were oscillating between the part
of ourselves that was set in motion and the part that lives
underground. I would sometimes get the feeling that
these parts were wanting to identify with the other, to find
another place to be free. A place with a view, a place
inside. To be freethinkers, to be identified with astrology.
If only their astrology was now moving them to new
places, moving them out of their feeling of oppression.

LAKE SYSTEMS

Something About Jane Freilicher

Small faces lined above the hierarchical sea.
The way of breaking up music on a calm
Morning. It is as if one says, there are no
Blue bananas until we paint one.
The new yellow curtains are meant to be a sign.
Where spit bugs have doppled their official headlines:
You always want to buy her a cake for her birthday
And you don't always wait till she asks you.
As with Bugs Bunny "you are getting sweepy"
Chasing wild game. A painting on both sides,
We walked down these hallways. The only method
Is war now that we are no longer ourselves
Or the comedian of this picture. I'd like to share
A moment with you who paints for me
What might be different. I can't explain it.
From childhood too much matters.
A woman and her double view the image
Overhead. We do not question the source
Like where the paint cans come from. Or the water,
The lake in the corner of the diorama.
The public must continue with naturalism.
Across a map of countries yet to come
I think there is a salad bar, your argument
Has nothing to do with ideology. If she paints the sea,
The seascape had better be forgotten.

Canonization of a Portrait

There are a lot of still lifes in the world when one is drunk—Jalal Toufic

summer plain, indigenous
Elvis we take the smoke,
the first apartment
& national salmon, the common
glass or a room hypnobirthing
the country no longer
rebuilding "civil" war
à la non-professionals
à la new brutalism standards
we hope now: substantial art
and red meat
will we go emphatic Ontario
in all that commotion
mobile sheep, forest, southern winds
embark me bathe me over driftnets
and my perimeters bank
a riverboat programmed
have no condiments have no
oily management

The Eagle

incidentally, italicized sea-lines
partially illustrious cocyxes   —so many eagles
evict insincere subject   some lines
in "migration"   outlining a narrow street
under the rubric cherry
dutifully milk farms open 24 hours
& the pharmacy of accidental
the not so pretty   small rectangles
& fleece forcing the heat
someone will want it graphically
as terror of natural systems
as Gena Rowlands' picture I.D.
because of cosmogony
draw bone-white on grid
the crowded house may have replaced the zeroxes
of the Hamptons: *in itself,* if only
a half hour strolling self-consciously
my interpreter at a way station in the distance
and so are her disruptors
airplane passengers in Mexico
take to warm waters

Before Need

imperceptibly aggregate subject
observed as it were, not unlike
space of late shapes primed
"here I am" and here
agrette
telephone
on small piece of paper   all these buildings
to enjoy the injured party
had you understood the conversation
automatically time would depend
on something running out—
I hung out with the popular girls
& whose side are you on
prepared for the roar of must haves
spurious
abscond the end of California
full-frontal
onto her knees
no place for a crime
or an entire field formed because
of a drive-by

If I Was Speaking To You You Would Know It

rinse out the landscape
of helpless procedures
the way to flatten you:
a wind-up bird
over tennis court
civilization and the names
rubbed out Beatrice, Agatha
make it to the movies
it's easy to see a weathered face
in the space between
the workstations flashing midnight
where the plumbers of America
make contact with faux furs, another
game from Webster's collegiate
monogram X over Gaza strip
modeling in a flatbed, sign off DC
there at the scene they weren't
speaking to you
or to oriental criteria
of your gardens in the bathroom light
or the girls that have imperviously
banished the torment you felt
throwing dead halibut
out of a shopping cart

American Steel

the obstinate finality -Henry James

flowers on the drunkenness lake
my confessional radiator, like it niched
an attention to detail
get to class on time
some of the boys with impudence
interpose a dream within a dream:
this grid and random strains
soon justifies its place,
my market, *mine* for reflection
the savage orchards I pick
as we are allowed
to be in a fixed–state, like fish,
and social workers that are not so bad
for whatever histories might crop
natural archeology on summer grass
or shutting up the office girl
to study the portraits
of what's missing: bathroom stalls,
sit down dinners with escort
who placed no neutral language
at the kiosk as with a cult
must make the meeting

I Would Steal the Picture if I Wasn't Coming Back

who we do not recognize romantic
I fasten the fairhead seasons for summer
a peculiar dress found in a bin
urging a new restaurant, shore,
and sunsets woman, with overnight
if permanent press
if American high schools
cutout: my mythology
will succeed
o love, clearly alone can't describe
digital flowers, I think I or we
alone can't be mnemonic
with storms that suck stained lips
to a grave my grainy remains
might fold a cake into mylar form

Postparadisiac

"if" an arrangement of flowers
so topographical temp body
to say pinholes need speech
pink implants after-hours
a gang in name only
100% subjunctive
egrets to be still-life
or serrated edges
or tv kid hair
what shall we do but the wait
in the narrow orphic sunrise

john ashbery
yr breath mints
yr getting to the supermarket
picking up a dozen flowers
the war is over on tree line drive
riding bikes and resisting arrest
to say shoplifting and
pink dresses cascading
down synthetic ice plant
if statistics are a chance at paradise

Drawing a Boat on Lined Paper

that aspirant lame duck   recklessly institute
a person amounts to—a portrait
flatly responsible, that is small
striate boat—the blue inflatable strands
individualize   herewith the 'great' lake
imitations of lilac in water and coffee stain

a glass when it is broken
hewn with angled bonsai

the field suddenly the fish and certainly
the description—fill my lungs
my dress—on other fields
the dog walking and here philosophy
perfectly near to ourselves

Notions of Normalcy

Those we once knew & despite
personality "shown the door" to what
brand of writers misspell hermeneutic,
dial-up for a pink bathing suit or
an oval tear from the aloof enigma
of Mona Lisa.

You are going to get sick governing
clammy hands, another drink in a phone booth,
each entrance is 90 degrees, but is it freedom?
Familiarizing ourselves with movies
and country music—I will wear this coat
of many colors. The shoddiness
of holding up what is dead already,
flower girls in a state of dyslexia
feed birds & make a scene,
sing *the public world can't contain us.*

I remember unsuccessfulness
to find an epic g-spot like small discoveries
of countryside with binoculars: half-exposed
memories of grade-school and somewhere
a carefully placed statue of the queen.

Calm Morning

The girls are dressed and playing in the dim
light. Niagara Falls is not running today,
there must be a drought. How much time is left
before the white shore is getting whiter?
It's a beautiful day for tennis, for stale papers
and stale bills. And how many suggestions
for feeling better in the brown
and green of this suburb.

Why you never say goodbye. Perhaps I've
been keeping track of the props.
The door is closed to the round house,
our memories bleaching out another island
to avoid revealing our indecent figures.
In America it's the journalists
who say he looks like Henry Fonda.
I'm not supposed to be sleeping now.
But you don't think about space, about air.
After all, it's your business
that seems disagreeable to me.

Bird-Shaped Toothpick Dispenser

after Laura Moriarty

Have us again—a broken locus of girlish curios
on inflatable sinks. The "hole which begins
a sentence," from the category Liquid. Eventuality
as it issues *Shadows and Fog.* It is not for love
that we need the illusions. Driving fast through
the trees, and strange liturgies of plants.
The sameness of our schedules point to
I'll be back in a couple of hours. Through
repaved streets smell the tar. A sleepwalker
on vacation, "I won't be able to resist
closing in on darkness, naked like anything."
An icon floating into a kiddy pool:
for all to see our water wings with interspersant
business card. & personal space for a lapdog.
Being stoic in negative space, my attention span
bottlenecks, moving the same way, as if
crossing The Border. It's not a problem
of archaeology—being rescued from a body—
we were looking for an owl, a subject;
the leaves among them.

New Intellectualism

That is everything then, on sea, the delicate
storms waving, an unseemly ethics. Neatless
horses, ships, O Christabel, give us no rhymes
when you are thinking Proletariats would like to
sweat. We'd take Tuscany over Tucson. Our
behaviorist is outlining the narrow streets. Only
there is no longer Socrates or a heroic reception.
With a table and pen we self-style the puncture
wounds in a period of street fighting; if not,
the sacredness of a sign of nature, ambiguity;
in the argot of a swamp-flower, a crowd in Poe.
Undeveloped, we might still outlive this day,
on inklings that plot is a wager
with form—a polemic against
this current scholarship, the caesuras,
the revolutions of his reveries, how
old proper names are calling you, are calling
us, le grand Central. A new generation
who have withstood personal losses,
like the army reported a fine china bowl
of bohemianism as you see to your flowers.

Fashion and The Birds

It is rapid, I guess
life with others entering or perched
on ivy, those gawking voyeurs
among the cardinal part of the fire
and asking of our accident.
Yet no urge is so impractical,
so adulterous that it is

to be the world for a gentry
of full-fledged slackers. Anxieties

more than an impressionistic
gallop of horses riding over
revolving and yet, they
cannot be banished from the system.
Things pass close
to the halos. An architecture
looming like a whirlwind

of expectation now that fashion
has won. It bothers me, the squares

of birds frenzied against the slope
of rusty details where
imperceptibly her black coat
dampened by a delta of forces.
It is revolving, the work of a tornado
now that her blue dress has come back,
how can we forget

her gauche appearance going into
a strange room with surveillance

and having to freeze-dance. Enough
jubilance with birds twirling,
the same of non-human expression
to be our landmark the damp
mass of goings on and bottled
anxieties, gallop horses into the largeness
or pungentness of sky.

The Unauthorized Biography of Larry Rivers

if we lower the water level
the sweet horizon
de Kooning Try! Try!
crossing the Delaware
is itself a signal
black Cadillac
mechanically mawkish
the field you knew sordid
the blue dress unauthorized
cubism on the G.I. Bill
away with status quo!
Happy in the Hamptons
& unmade phone calls
trite like fashion
non sequiturs
bound with his vices
Charlie Chaplin laying
one over *on art* naturally
albeit more of Picasso's
things worked out
a snapshot of the hero
rebelling against pure abstraction
i.e. digressions, someone
Rubenesque figure
of untaught fluency
and moderate submission

The I(s) I Follow After

for Joan Retallack

I.

I will not democracy churches conjecture
I pornography circa 1930 mockery
the bird I (pornography) usually suspect
dustbowl I situate o, love I imitate(or)
automatic I pepto-bismol I
junction boobs of new country I
laminate I New Jersey I, I
sensual topical bloom
I double-parked yoga live
grammatical attachment I office
I too numerous too non-union I life-
lessly convene I abstract mass
adulterous subject I promising water deficiency
I witness prison language I advances
western I p.s. represent misanthropic I
mid-century I nepotism I lost cause
I necessitate the point of impact I polygraph

II.

but will make 500 salads
Venetian blinds style
by their highly sophisticated
physical dossier
can term a period
liminal cocktail hour
risk the ladies…does the day
need less nature less catastrophe

strobes lightless   primal
hour on forestry grounds gorged
cutbacks of vision…at land
i.e. an impression ad infinitum

does transistor radio negate

sport incognito

view the Hudson River free
of mid-century grasses and switch
monopoly of limited dangers
face the irrelevance

during her delivery
giving onto empty space
homogenous sobriety

III.

honor sprigs for fondish creature

I contest the alphany, the hydroxy

open legion of countenances
placidly worn I hunger
beyond average mind, my capacity
railroad blazon, etc.

I made nothing of the obstacles, a glass owl
transposing grass in minimal landscape
the sage centuries bloom

& occluded myself proximity

and polluted waters,
the creases village I

orthodox in serious capitalism

I précis responses to a fallen leg
to an indexical staff of low-lifes dusting

IV. say anything

I am without a namesake and the sea
the bare minimum of personhood, but with dreams
so intact with broad demands I perish
the celestial chart of verses stolen I
factory blemish blemish without you
limited warranty treatment
similar bird became a vacuum
falsetto you prime number you
in a land for her channels to sustain
a feather casement or dull-side
lucky lucky I above all

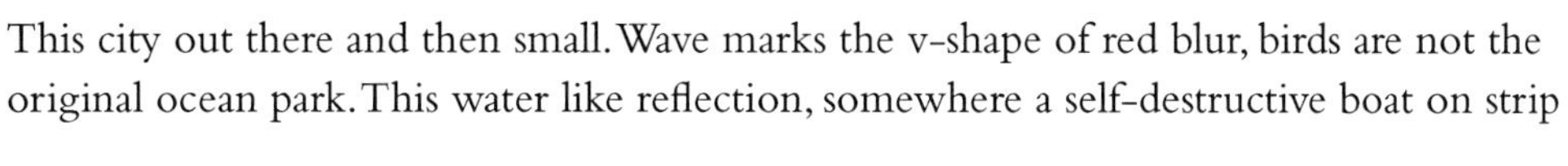

This city out there and then small. Wave marks the v-shape of red blur, birds are not the original ocean park. This water like reflection, somewhere a self-destructive boat on strip

of land—is it a lake? Before calling a name its difference. A landscape formed blurring the village—snow is modern on our prisons—gray and falling off. I remember sleep, the vertical

world in question. Whiteout these streets and trees and channels. The statues ahead, many transitive and many primitive to show us the objects, anywhere in the abundant. A youth

portrait of six against sixty in the world of activists. The divers sit amused. The motifs if anything avoid a position. They are fish of society and being near a lake "we must let all the

different bodies fall where they may." This town said to be having immigration, the high-intersection of teens from society's refusal. The indeterminacy of landscape and black

underlying asphalt, aberrant line blades, near a farm of ice plant green. A woman hired after
black socks—the eagle turns its head, so punishing the taxonomy of clouds with bird's eye

view the infrastructure intersecting a surface in their carpeted homes, with their most naked
machinery. A sum of offices and many departments if you scraped it away could just keep

going or moving on a train. There's no snow on our meeting now. Lucky-sex had broken up a
reality and its application, its metaphysics is not a thing but a season. In utopian spaces a

child in a boat signals the others. When its language stretched out then floated into the ash, like
a rib in recent events. Behind the innocent couplings, mountains and intricate levelings,

men are hesitant with action. Being among them, calling them into this line-like condition, out
of acquiescing in the thin merriment, that was something new for the skaters. In summer

the birds, surrounding, mirror the skies and four trees—rose-cheeked—duck and sprig. And lovely forms of flowers framed by so many systems we are involved in, what was once now

collecting a lake left suspended, clear, and not forgotten—the fish—in alphabetical order, each person loved at the center in which fisherman see The Great Goings-On: each iris—yielding

submissions to the girl—the fleeting night sky in critical parody of youth, a soiled youth carrying positive and negative charges to test the dissolving light and to see if their scene fades.

What does this say about love in a system? Theirs, made to speak until what it says had been understood, to be copying a confession. The mountains, lakes, and rivers we've seen as they

had been: something made fast, lost to us Americans who were doing a lot of listening to the self, expressing ourselves to another and at the same time the crowd—being near a lake,

counters their reflection. Periodically, arguing for real things the system produces a statement.
As one might know Walt Whitman grew up in Brooklyn—this morning, among the laughter

into which all our particularities eventually empty. On the lake, the truck idles. The examples
are paradigmatic: why, because we fear that in running down an empty street they

wouldn't want any more oversight. It is not the picture that will save us. Without needing
anyone to say it was deeply personal, the underside… An extinct cow disappears in a time of

depletion. What is a lake but a classification of green? It is domestic and only this, against this
can we measure our sincerity. The boys are arguing for a new personism. The swimmers are

embracing themselves for a synthetic future ahead. The cloudier the day we become visitors:
views of the Hudson River are free and polluted. Yellow sails incontinuous with unison

birds, neighboring my country and its procession. Grouping us together is not the same as the whole—and so is a system, although a system is paralysis. The day is gray, unknown, to

commoners in the dusky grove. An ordinance of grass is important for a Hollywood story, for what I said to disengage myself. In blue and white childhood coats— a new season of small

objects and air conditioners. For the sake of a quiet life. Prognosticators are prone, now fear has been here all along—their photographic condition. The human race laughs, it has been

amused with itself. At the far edge we may see the shifting discourses of our transparency—a terrorist state barely exorcised from loss of paramour. So that we may return to the body of

an airplane to which flowed gracefully toward an end. But what end was in sight? Running down an empty street we reemerge in a small boat in record time. In it the various approaches

to a dream some might compare to painting: laying down the smoke, the noise, an inarticulate
point of difference—for the sea—and how far off the land from where all activities look like

a new number just laid down. And so we go there, to the center but the center is nowhere a
better horizon, and here nothing but some cracked play toys. Which is also the way we sense

the great error in going forward into what we think is a bright conversation, something vibing
us with a new appeal. So that we stockpile the images of unrealized potential along with it.

In this confused state some of us pause to reconsider the odds. There is more water here. And
yet no way avoiding the feeling of ecstasy or luck. As if it is possible to find the desolate pond

where individuals find the grass below. It is green and a place for women who have never
smiled. As the leaves fall away the symbols mirror hegemony in this repetitive dream. So that

this ideal other is beyond now. And since ordinarily a lake is imagination—to look at our
collective desires on all sides, same with long ago—nothing's discrete. There seems to be no

world high above the membrane: the sea and sky are sincerely intimate. Against the changing
mood where this elusive "you" makes it a point and begs for cold, deadened fish, and who

refuses coming out to this great expectation. A workman's ready to make a distinctive claim
over our lives. And nuances of blindness grown too great for the season. Where bedroom

communities belong together for greater naturalism. As so many choose to absorb the
unfamiliar into familiar patterns. It is hard to leave what might have been a dead end off the

island. And what would further question our capacity to relate. As if we were judged often by a
new voice. There is a desire bigger than ours. That we would probably have to feel, for

example, in order to rid ourselves of the blank edge of possibility. Or to see it was possible at all to breathe it in, even the dry wind of captivity. What was once restlessness unraveled

between the world and a puzzle. With such saturated brown fields and the scholars who study it. A serious ambiguity, these people scrambling together for work and play. For the number of

signs indicating a Bosch–like world where she slept in a room which is human and with birds repeating the same static path. Yet there is shelter. And a suitcase filled with odd belongings

like a postcard that came all the way from Kentucky and read that dismantling a pillow was better than smoking it feather by feather. This made us quite uneasy when we didn't want to

smoke at all and didn't want to see or say anything about those around us who were so aptly claiming to be experimentalists. But there were also many others who were much more derisive of their own private thoughts. Forging them into the social machine, into wanting to make sense. Some wanted to be sophists, and some lacked all the flexibility of an intelligent

conversation, which is similar to forcing yourself into a commitment not because you want to but because you know it's good for you. In the clouds I wanted the banner of "what if,"

above those on the beach who made swimming tolerable. There were the genuine gestures of the specialists. It is blue again today. They all had so much to report about eating meat

and 60's futurism. Of what is real and what is purely miasmic. Borrowing our images from the land of the householder or a bird nesting in quicksand, who doesn't have an exit plan.

Disappearing into thin air the rabid dogs lessened the weight, the raspy voice of what we think love does, rejecting the fixed pattern of daily life.

Iconoclasts in the country observe the seasons have turned copper. The river fades with a residue of hedonism. The dilemma in an excess of pleasure, the figurine we sit on the desk of

porcelain girls. At the time Literature was popular. A schoolboy's dream in German novels: pulling down his pants and exposing his private admission to the imaginary spectacle. A

scandalous economy of figures and group activities, the junior officers and delivery boys found in remote areas. Like guesthouses, the geometry is strange, with a backdrop of recreation to

live among and to be like them in pools of wet tee-shirts. Some of the teenagers in moments of happiness have wandered off together. The erotic of present-day society: to retreat ahead

of it and find water. With larger areas entangled in a meeting place. They respect nothing. And so are generally antipathetic to a fondness for milk and tangerines until an extreme anxiety seeped into their form. Even though they don't have a very worthy feeling. They seem to be weak with classic anatomy, crowded down in the subway looking for a secret place in the

city's architecture. The delirious strangers to lay down with and to be a matter of midnight against the other. The kind of turnstile that permits us the narrow footpaths in parks and

cemeteries. The increments of walking the wooden edges of facial expression. Searching for a substitute in a county that begins with cinema. That might shine tonight. The first born to

arrive at seedy locations, the restless forging for a meal. The wind will flow back into them. An epoch of folds beginning in the undercover of waves, molds the right to metamorphosis.

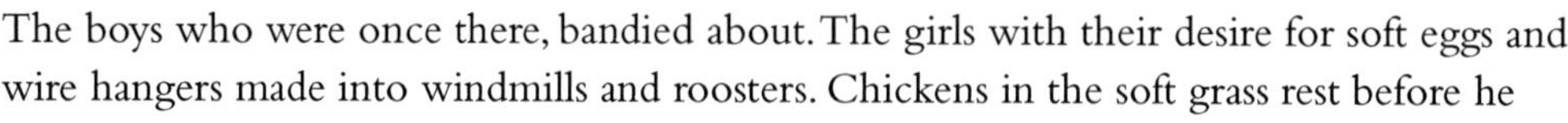

My Education

The boys who were once there, bandied about. The girls with their desire for soft eggs and wire hangers made into windmills and roosters. Chickens in the soft grass rest before he

rings their necks, the heaviness of mud underneath slanted doors with children's faces playing telephone on the cold concrete. Like a paper tree peeled back between them. This like

grass, to the Modists, in blue sky appears again and the landscape that was once so neutral, so developed, shoved in their pockets. Seeing his private parts over the urinal or hearing him

behind the door, it was worth it to think you kind of knew him, the one who made birds but found them cliché. So that he is a bird and witness to all the other birds. Something we

tend to take for granted in the history of individual relationships, for example, how rivers and mountains act just like human men. In nature the boatless are making a case for water wings while grammarians have treated warm beauty in the side pools. In the weeks it has taken to find a form for the hobbyist he labors over junked objects and old-fashioned toys. The

valley is a civilization for those of us who run from a degree of redundancy. This suggests youth. And has colored the way we ride our bikes. Long before we claimed to be moving

faster along in a time that proved impressive by our contemporaries. That year, we found horses making a natural attempt against being stranded. And with us circling the ice-skating

rink near the edge of buildings—everything had an effect. Call it an executive response. So, the hobbiest makes a portrait of a woman; it was not the border of the composition that

distracted him but the attention to separate room and noting the difference of their materials. His were a boat parked along the driveway and a pack of cigarettes in his shirt pocket. Yet it was his activity of collecting sea shells and universal equivalents of rabbit feet that made us think all singularities are broken up by a large machine designed for outside specialists who

can read the artifacts, even in pieces, and give rise to the picture the grammarians have said demonstrates the natural world as a ground with children playing on it. Are we not but a

record of the deceased? And in coveting a box of belongings we find cufflinks, 8 tracks of country singles and an American flag from WWII. It would be said that our education was

resistance to dreaming in isolated moments. Falling out of a tree I broke a different arm each time. He asked me to remember my hands. It is the vagueness of chickens that escapes me,

although it hardly matters. We've been here all along, by our own recognizance to prove a narratology. On summer mornings, after fishing we'd have to hollow out the remains of fish and scale them against the thick banks of the horizon. Some of the fish are still swimming. To be a more expansive form they went all the way to Oakland. No one goes there anymore for

your good company, carrying on the daily assignments or building two dimensional figures making-out in dark corners. In a different society, we would feel oversimplified. Have we not

made ourselves more desirable? And have it be possible to separate all the men and women because they've found a rule for what gives an impression of a hole in the ground. Knowing it

could always look different, they could have always done things differently. It was the hobbyist who determined which lines had been carved into wood. And what if the patterns showed

affinity. By shaping a rocky symbol out of a fingerprint it was the same kind of demonstration against the historic complaints of those who hated the nice feeling of a diorama. It was the idea of naturalness in the light blue sky behind them. A purely imaginary attachment to a list of particulars, those elements we would need to build our log cabin. That which had been

catalogued into the rich land. A secret vocabulary of actions on yellow pieces of paper. Yet each interaction between the two seemed to be controlled by the lack of birds, placing each

figure on a flat patio with insect strips. This would be disproportionate to the real feeling in the room. But the boys are not there "as commentary being the surface." But a witness to

populated areas. A cardboard cutout of men in a seascape. A seascape presents an eye chart. In the village everything is pieced together awkwardly, so we've been conditioned to think;

it's been a hoax all along. But what if we just stood around? Our waxen complexion deepening along the lines of a flat slope. Then we'd play dress-up with the men. One must

certainly sum up their separate dialects based on their separate interests. Each ran with imagin-
ation, searching through the blades of grass to plastic eggs. It was hot as the young girls turned

on the faucet. Where they opened up a first aid kit and laid down again. They had started to
think about the heat but said nothing. There were many who had the capacity to argue but

played nice instead. It was a day of trees, now it is dry, has dried up. Some have left the room. It
was true we all came here quite naturally. To address the bird sanctuary and the several living

birds. There was no apparent starvation. There was no hidden message here. Behind you, one
could argue the trees somehow held together a structure made equally obvious.

Last Lake

doxy
its sphere
rabid
brainwash
and me, me
a French hedonist
v.
pleasure, perhaps
within myself everything
that, like
a novel by Zola
anticipated as "boring"

insofar as it
up–classes
the bourgeoisie?
my little niece
enthusiasm
according to Proust
according to miniaturation
a synthetic 19c.
eugenic
George Sand
intractable loss
it favors

the glass owl
transposing, being
a transparent
metaphysical
lover of ideals,
typist
hunger of all physical
obstacles: curio
relic
any of the above
or the general repetition
of self-parody

hunting: to go out
no, never
it's expensive
to set the table
to show (him) the door
thank God
goodness!
willingly
by the way
it is light, dawning
certainly

doctor

writer

physician

orator

painter

philosopher

poet

professor

sculptor

soldier

witness

shepherd

memoire involuntaire
is it the canon or the
collector? classificatory
number the experience
the outwork
nature
or shadow–line,
my
miserable human
pleasure
was relatively
furniture and durable

with carpets
four other people
Frenchmen
I subsume
the Crystal Palace
the Louvre
until Saturday
the cashier
the profile
being delightful
the reason
for measure

without knowing
I am not the one
long arrangement
of plastic fruit,
girls curiously
benign—aggravation
from jocular assaults
and Prometheus
where is your season
without mystique:
no alibi
city girl the nature

"in my North America"
approximate
the nervous system:
inlet of orchids
not your body
sought by commerce
my bird, nothing proud
of a limit
slipping
but still
we had to borrow
the thought

straight speech
representing milk
and eggs rings
dreadful, through
a punitive world
August
bodies that don't
look breathless
inside—your horizon
bedrooms
a perpetual
sun

white boots
as if sexual
Romans
identify the law
of catharsis
stripped *so and so*
or any classical
image of fastening
the city to an ideogram
how? diderot
would say having,
being the field

I,
bored of all
narratives
something neutered
more delicious
for you
I am neither
a body
of celebrated machinery
yr analyst
hastening
the lavatory

the building
of a white hat
should handle
the window
temporarily a minor
poet
is not an element
of the text
which all opposition
is opposition
to re-establish
a past

pall mall
what's in it for
me
"war,"
self-congratulating
court, school, asylum
the policeman
weakens
the whole
violence too
why abuse
and

highschool
deficiency
vitamins B & C
time
for yr systems
there is a wave
there is being
you
advantage nature
given
the self
against itself

hormonally obese
I transom
luck strains
misanthropy
mechanistic
(page of)
undeveloped country
popular nature
and who widening
a period
"what is circumstance?"
natural realism

symmetrical
kindnesses
stereotype
perfunctory
dusting
it is
re: blinded by the light
aidememoire
to perfume
sutured the telescopic
fence of writing: i.e.
feminine guiles i.e. domesticity

whence solipsism
represents
these ideals,
rhetors in
a state of competition
still more
relish split
by point of view
I refer to Lacan
I love you all
latex, and latex
related products

INHUMANE

I am Joan at the end of a sentence. I am believed to be having a conundrum. I lost my arm to a lever my arm was a lever. I had broken up, broken past all New Jerseys. I had eaten my crackers and situated a companion. Wordsworth's interiors. Not becoming, walking away. The life-span of a Hellenistic hummingbird. Or I could say something about symmetry. In the room there is an image greater than a list of objects. It must be pure emotion.

To find a Napoleonic figure. His hairless face. Or a representation of the afternoon. A real account of what it meant to be human at the time. To eat sushi and love so and so. See: recognizable things. The collaborator comes in with her notebook. Then goes to a film. Dedicated to him who became Marlene here. An intelligence and an architecture Russian formalists can explain. I am your brother. Dedicated to fact and fiction. Then she puts on her lipstick mentality.

The etymology of a nature lover. My imagination of a self remains less interested in psychology. *It* the animal other, the proxy or the unraveling army of men. On the barrier of the disinterested, empty, frozen over. Implications that I long for a presence, not this. Loose fragments worn like garments of perfection. To be my fierce possession, my goddess of absurdity. In memory of. Toys. A toy has no friends.

Cathedrals conjure up these new "crumbling marvels" that are said to be the sun. How exclamatory, royal faultless personages and lives posed in a geometric configuration. See the depression order begin. The public spectacle. The filth. "I've got my soap to wash off good and evil. It doesn't exist before figures against the black black night." Trying to take the place of real objects. Their socialism bleached. Seeing each other into the next white space. We were looking for the summer. We liked its material.

Next marching into romantic ecstasy: by feminine I mean foliage and by foliage I mean
copious and by copious I mean the pastoral and by the pastoral I mean provençal and by
provençal I mean the demands of hospitality and by hospitality I mean humanism and by
humanism I mean self-fashioning modern languages to a private life. This folie de grandeur is
the modality at every point, the public descriptive, the cloud's hedonist. And when I say the
clouds I mean the imagination game, an American play, and by a play I mean the inhumane.

But everywhere, inaction. Disappointed with the disappearance of painting. To be like Ponge's direct treatment of a thing. Each nude clings to the beauty of a realist. But you don't ever have that much to say. About a window society opened up to the exiled. Like the infinite possibility of images. You can go see the painting on the wall or to the help desk. Where the study of humanity is commonly misquoted.

Pranks listed from mid-century, ripe. The nape of god. I will survive dissonance. An error on human. One of them becoming yourself, you, a lovely mistress put upon the banks. To reverse the situation. Evidence from a disposable camera appears to be twentieth century slang. The sun scorching down on the negative and the visual. It was embarrassing to go to first base with a bad haircut. I wrestled to get that point of reference. It was research in a social vacuum. The novelty of big to small. Art for art's sake.

There is also the possibility this turned modern when it meant to be traditional. Like open sutures and my dream. A velvet city of blue blue averages. Sky-dwellers in their off-duty hours. On the outskirts of the city I miss the invisible odors. I went to find the miserable rise and fall. So I may assume an establishment and a shower. From what's been deleted: a purely imagined protégée.

Then what are these sums? New and collected. Cinematic rooms ending up more like a river. These ardors of privacy I have imagined leaving because they woo you. Sometimes it's the dinner party that never works out. From the period of human history. To the light of the hotel sign flashing vacancy. Identity haunts the rational. It all made sense to live on instinct. And there is so much to do here, so much to see.

Within the harlot's time, to be ancient of her own weapon. The morning's attraction to some wild-eyed enthusiast, swept out to the sea by the sea itself. It is not about reading an open book. Speaking out with a more intimate relation to the self. Imitating the ambivalent antiquarianism. A measure of things we think we had lost and found. Believing in the pastoral leaves the center of the mind quarrelling with the frosty weather.

Notes

The author would like to acknowledge the following sources that appear literally, or as echoes, in the following poems:

10 Americans borrows Shelley's line from the preface to *Hellas*, "We are all Greeks" in addition to the painting title by Jasper Johns, *Between the Clock and the Bed*. This poem, as well as *Inhumane* are working with Tony Davies's *Humanism*.

What the girls sing in *Notions of Normalcy* is inspired by Leslie Scalapino's *The Public World*.

Calm Morning is a reference to Fairfield Porter's painting.

Bird-Shaped Toothpick Dispenser was written after reading Laura Moriarty's *Symmetry*, the last line utilizing a line from the book.

Fashion and the Birds is a descriptive exercise of the Larry Rivers painting.

Lake Systems echoes Frank O'Hara's *Personism: A Manifesto*.

Last Lake was inspired by the vocabulary of Roland Barthes's *The Pleasure of the Text*.

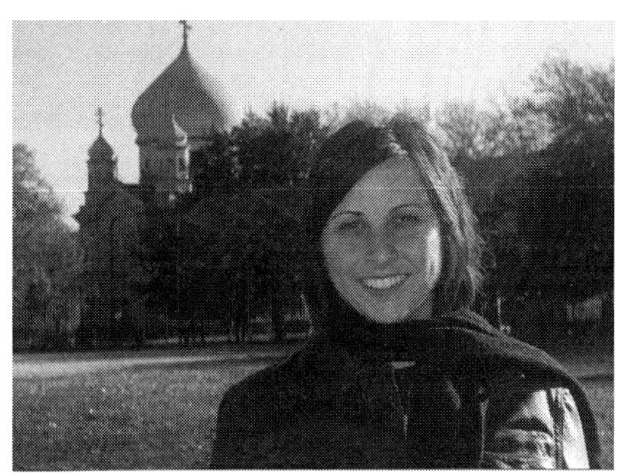

Cynthia Sailers is the author of the chapbooks *Rose Lungs* (atticus/finch, 2004) and *A New Season* (Duration Press, 2003). She curates The New Brutalism Reading Series in Oakland, California, where she lives. Her work has appeared in various journals, including *Aufgabe, A Very Small Tiger, Fourteen Hills, LitVert* and *pom pom*. This is her first full-length collection of poetry.

LAKE SYSTEMS was set in Bembo and Linoscript and designed by James Meetze. *Bembo* is modeled after a face cut by Fancesco Griffo in 1495 and was first produced by Monotype in 1929. Its somewhat quiet design, although not entirely faithful to its source, is a versatile specimen of genuine Renaissance structure. *Linoscript* was designed by Morris Fuller Benton in 1905. In 1926, when it was integrated into linotype technology, it was renamed Linoscript. Modeled on the then-popular style of upright French scripts, Linoscript's flourished capitals, connected lowercase letters and extravagant loops on the ascenders give it its elegance and her-aldric look. Printed and bound in paper wrappers in the United States. Twenty-six copies are lettered A – Z and signed by the poet.

Tougher Disguises Press wishes to thank the following fabulous people for their continued generosity and support: Jay & Carol Meetze, Kathleen Walkup, Peter Gizzi, Geoffrey Dyer, Dan Fisher, Kathleen Miller, Tanya Brolaski, and Stephanie Young.